THIS BOOK

BELONGS TO

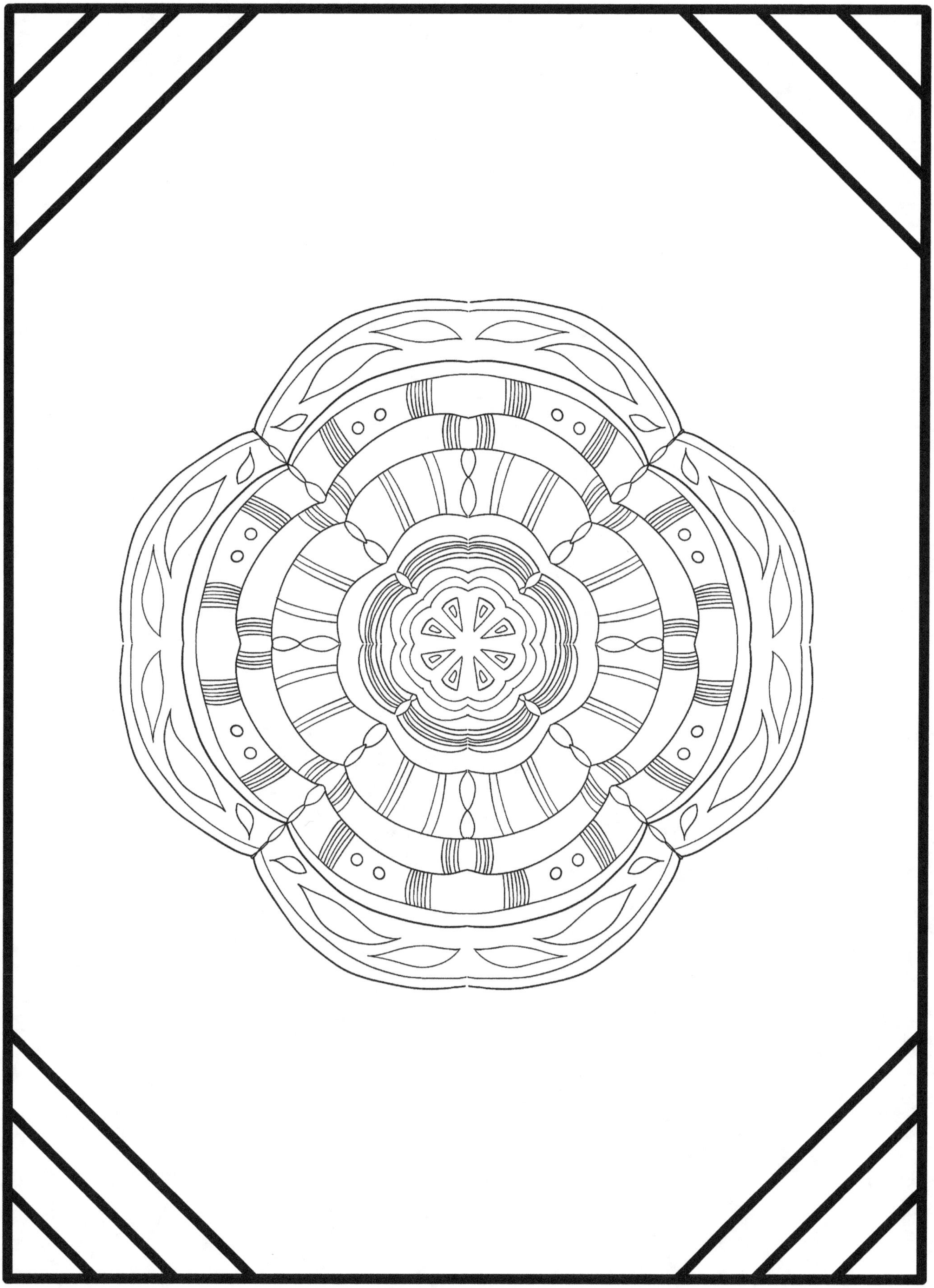

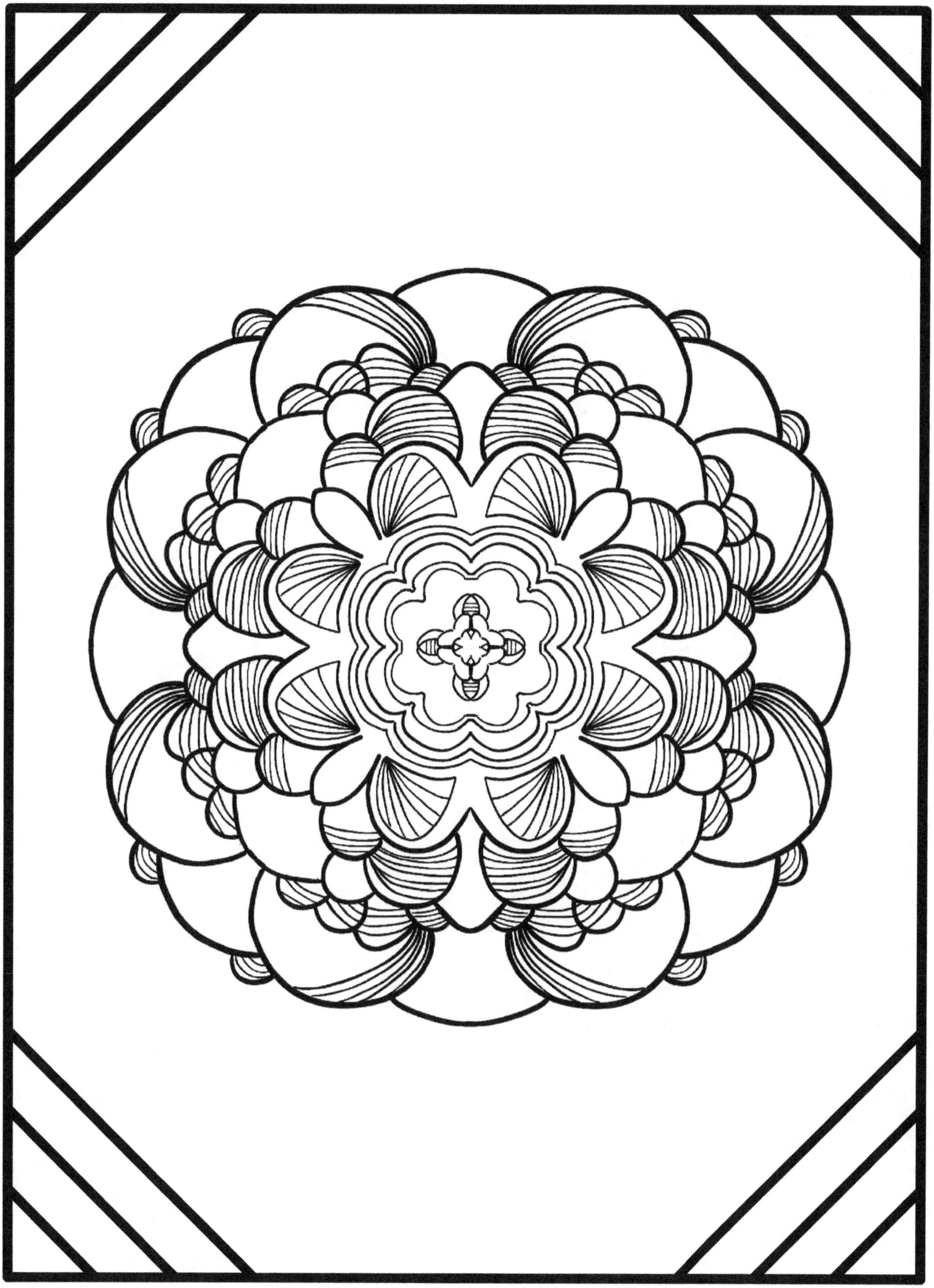

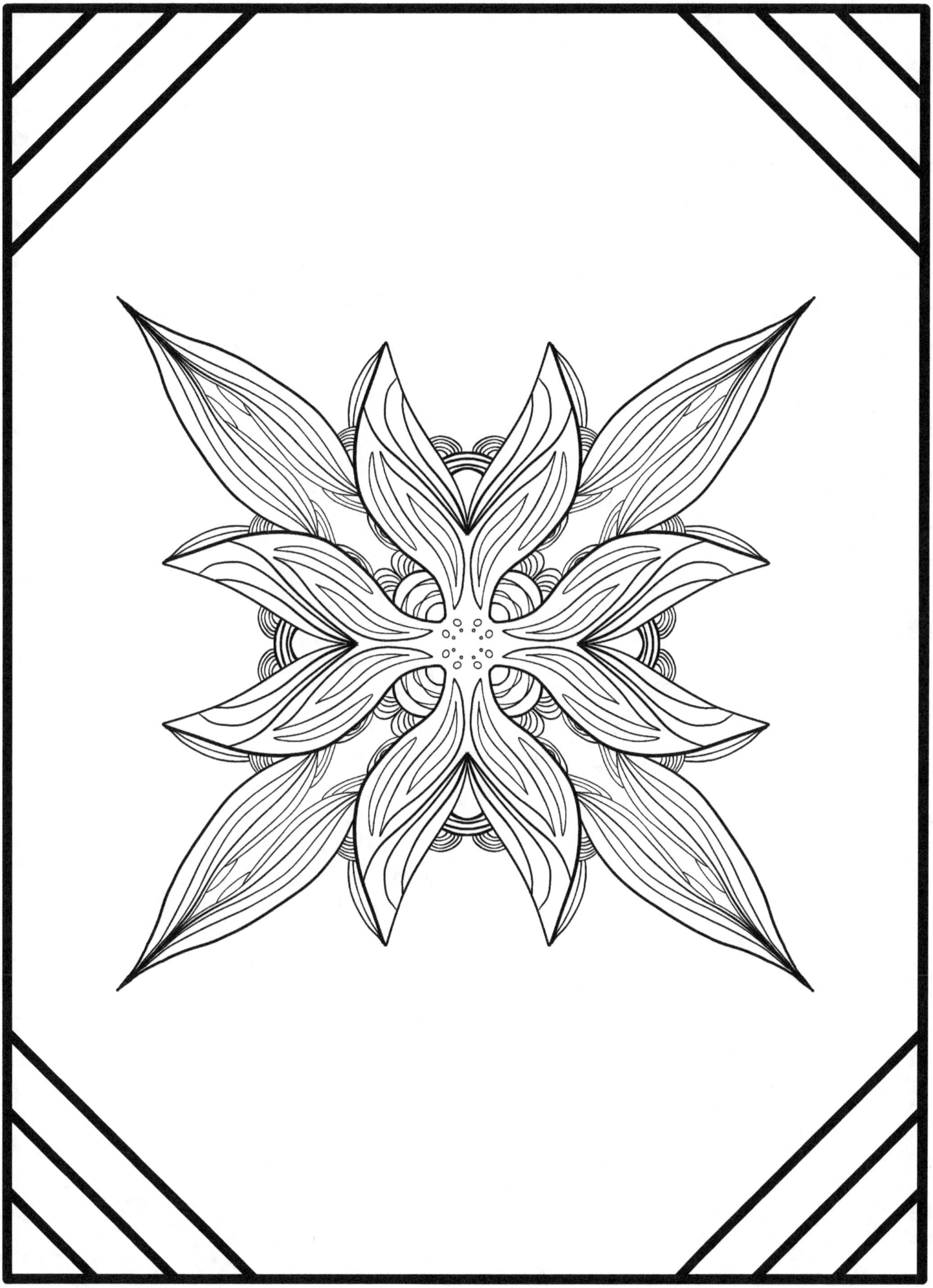

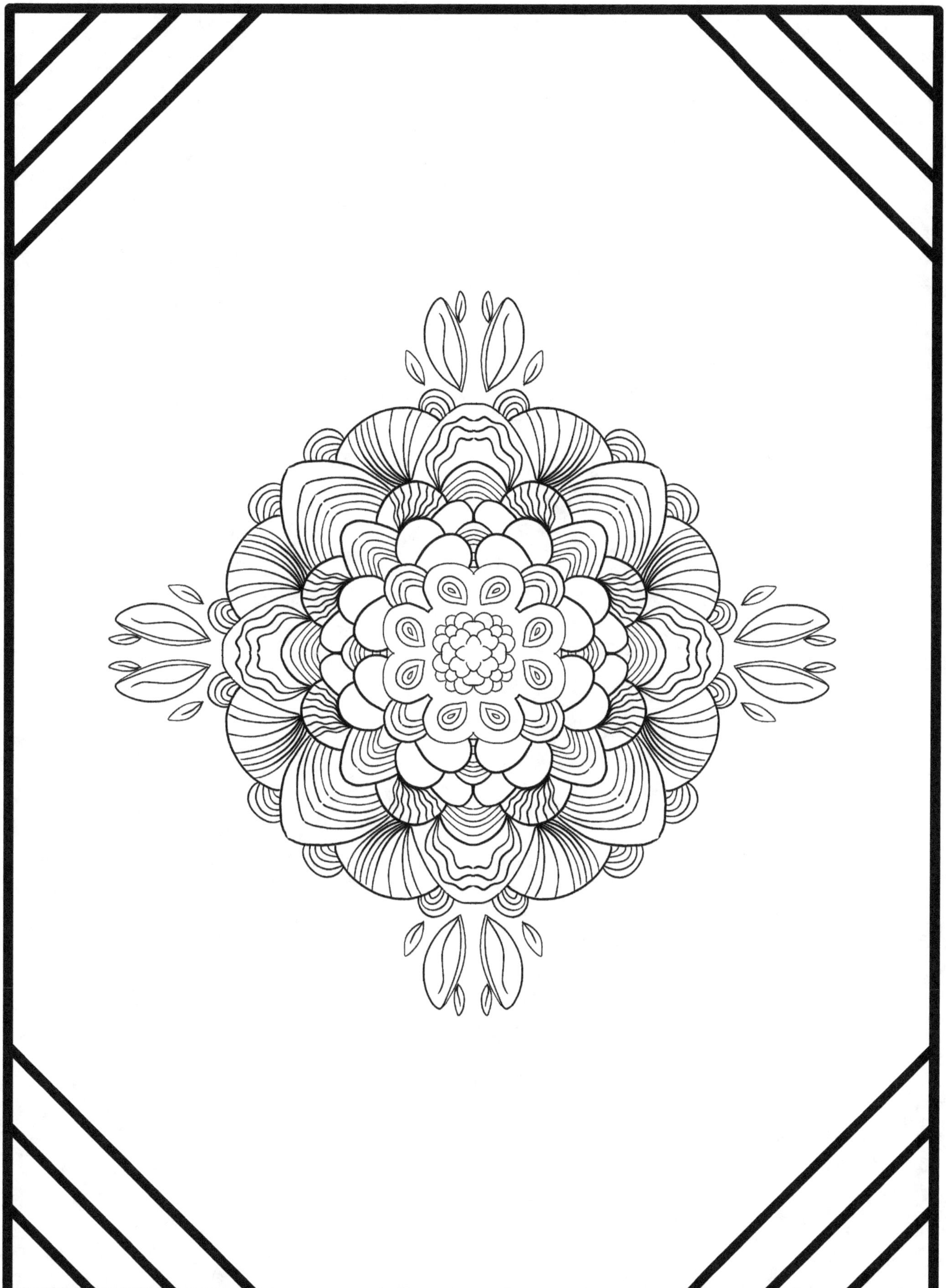

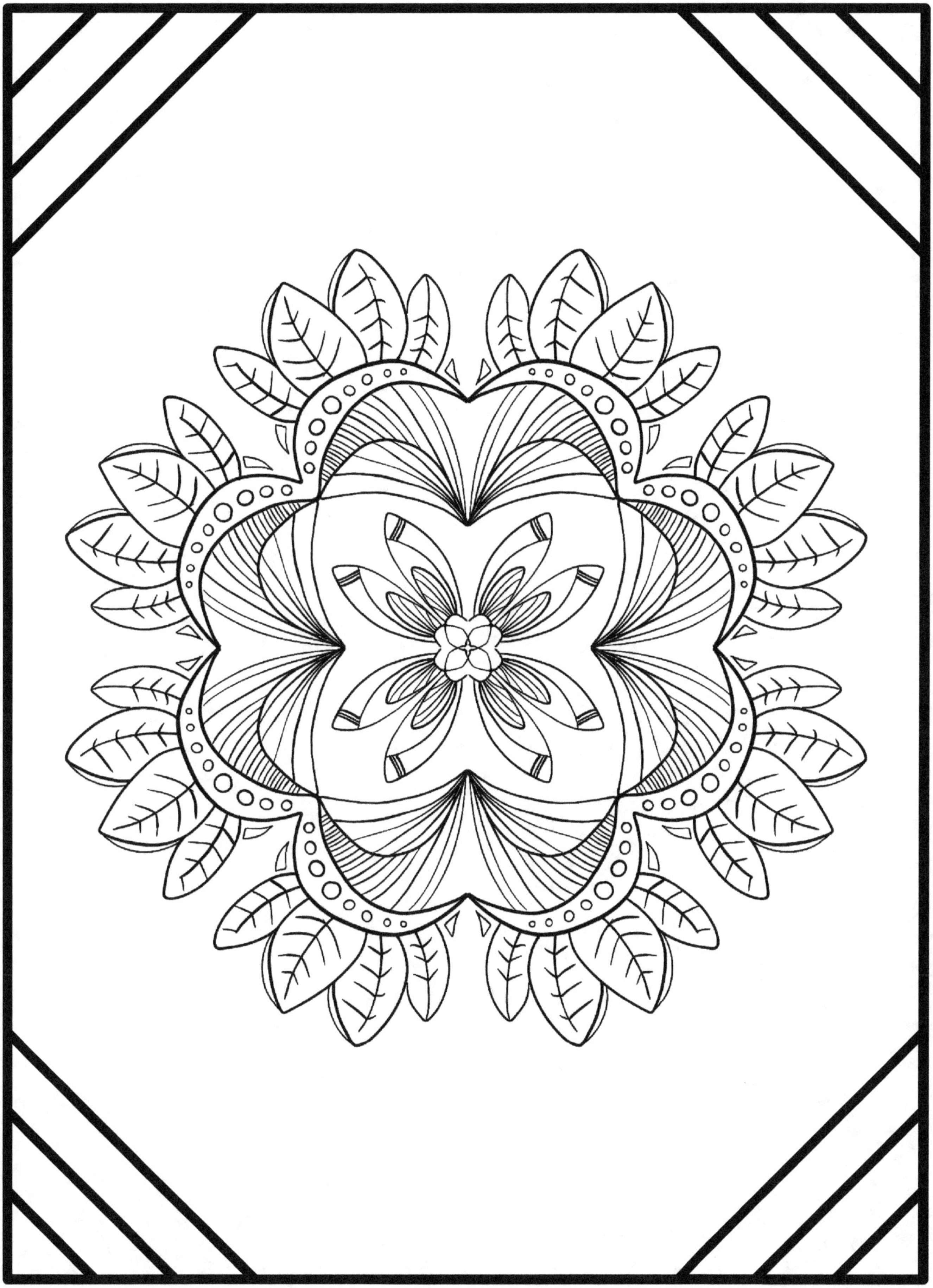

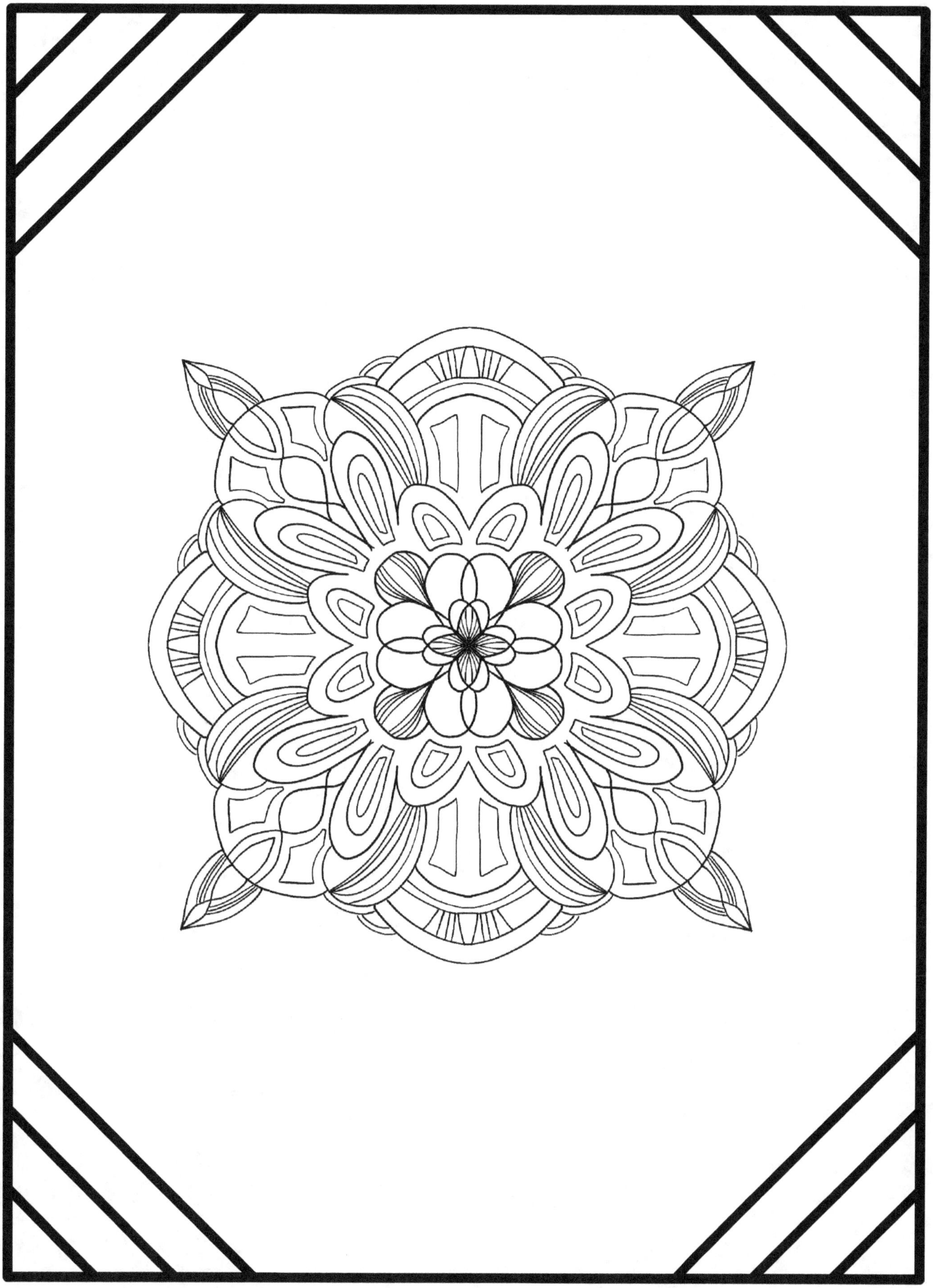

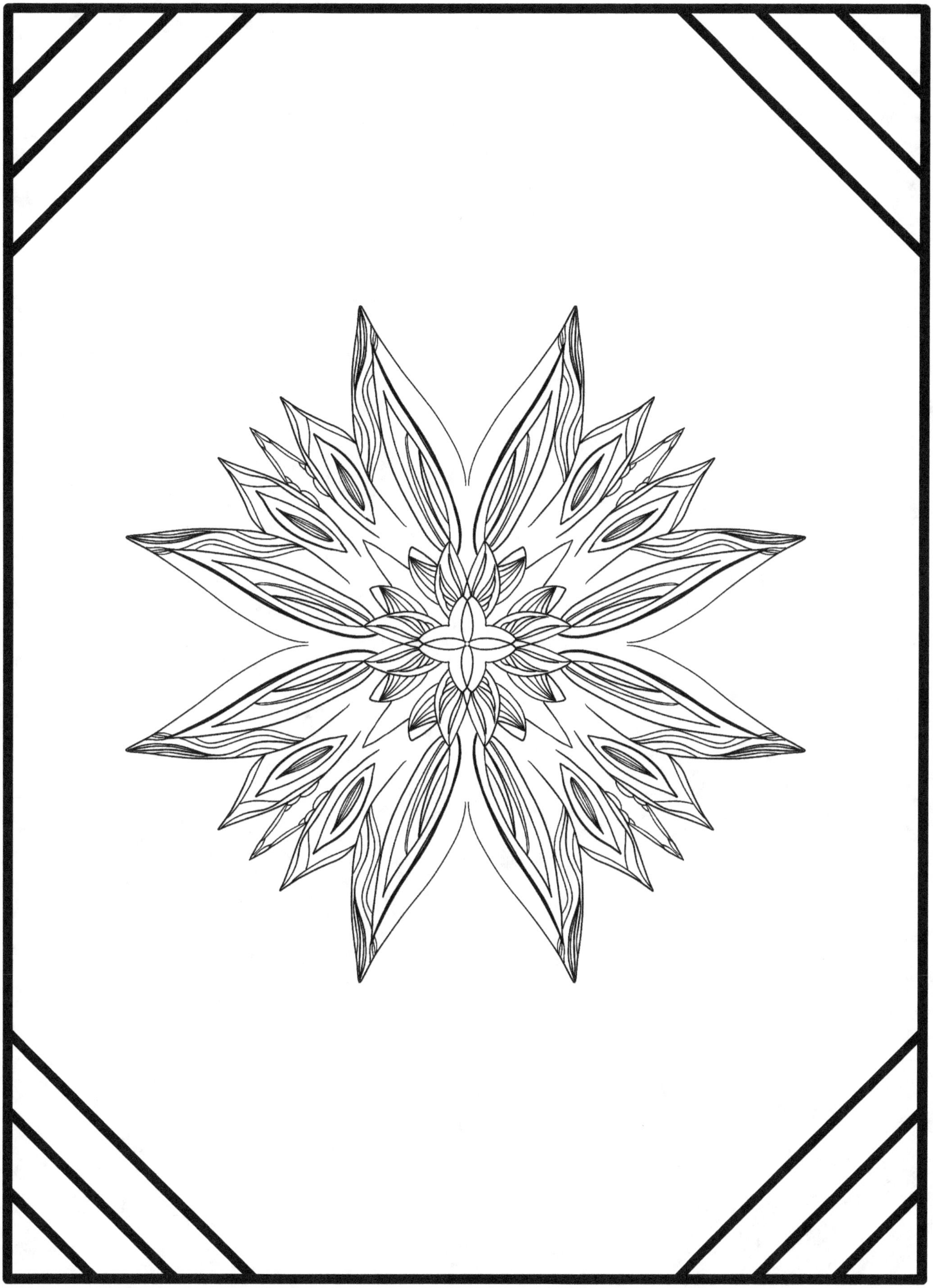

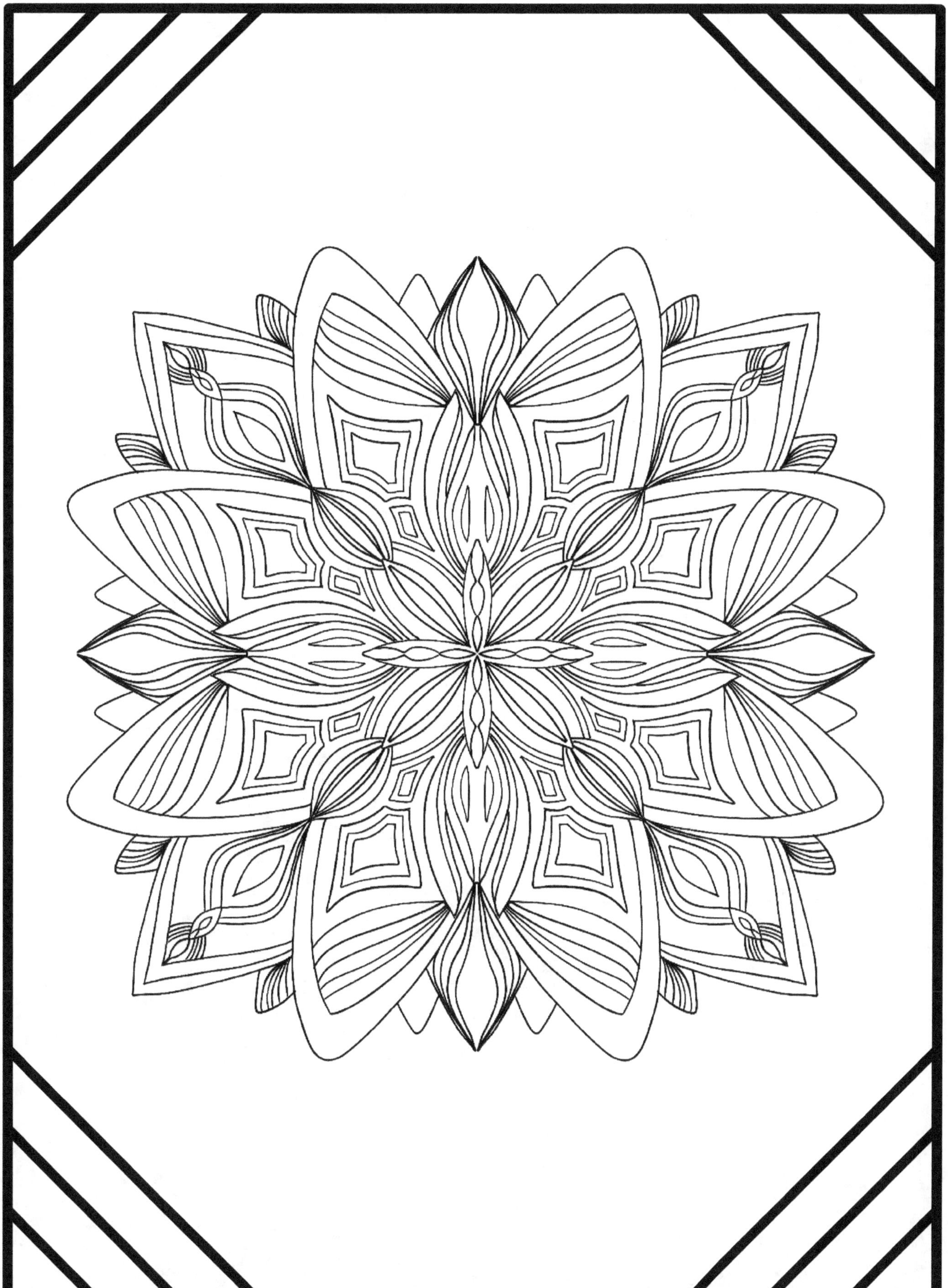

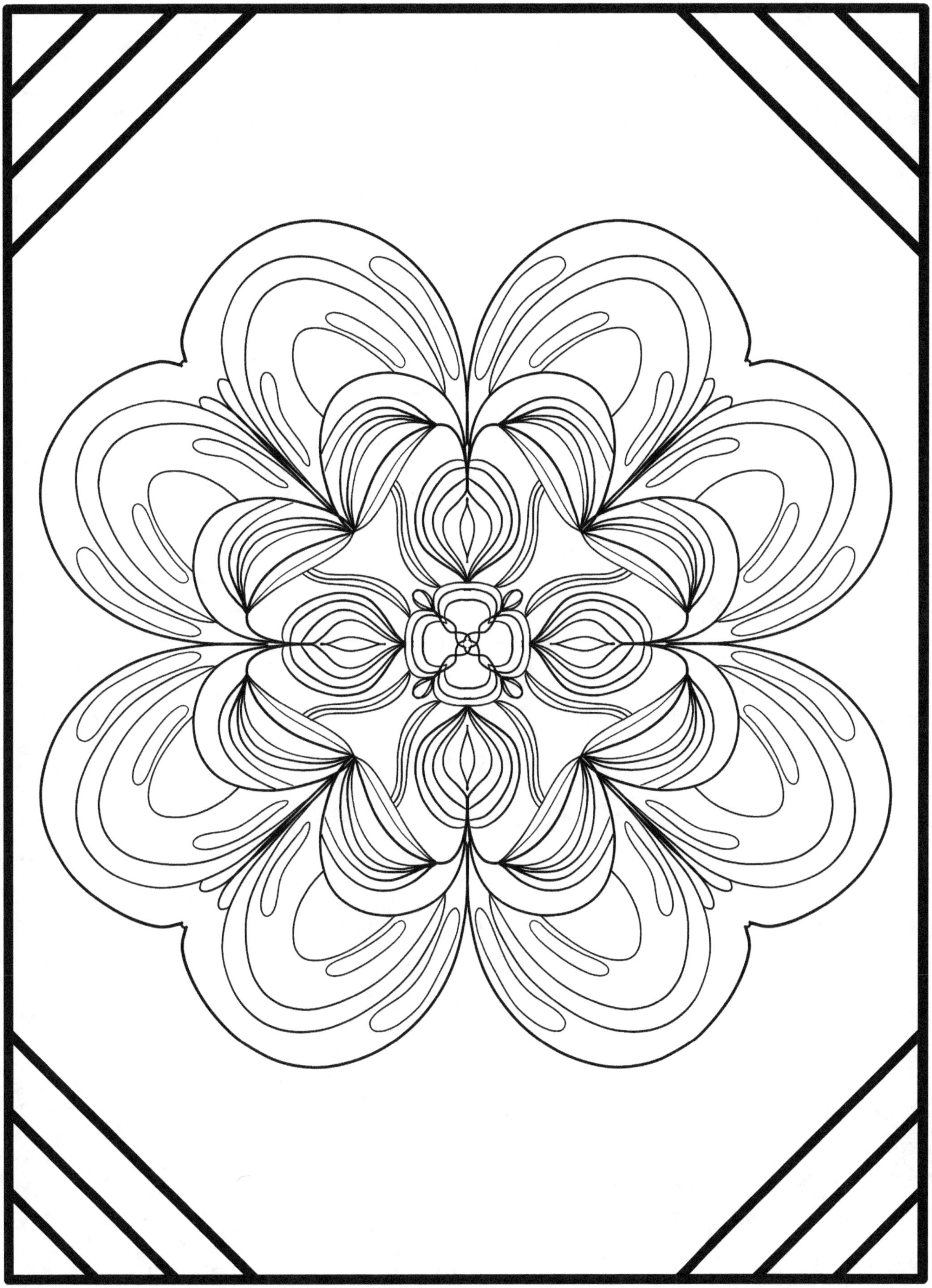

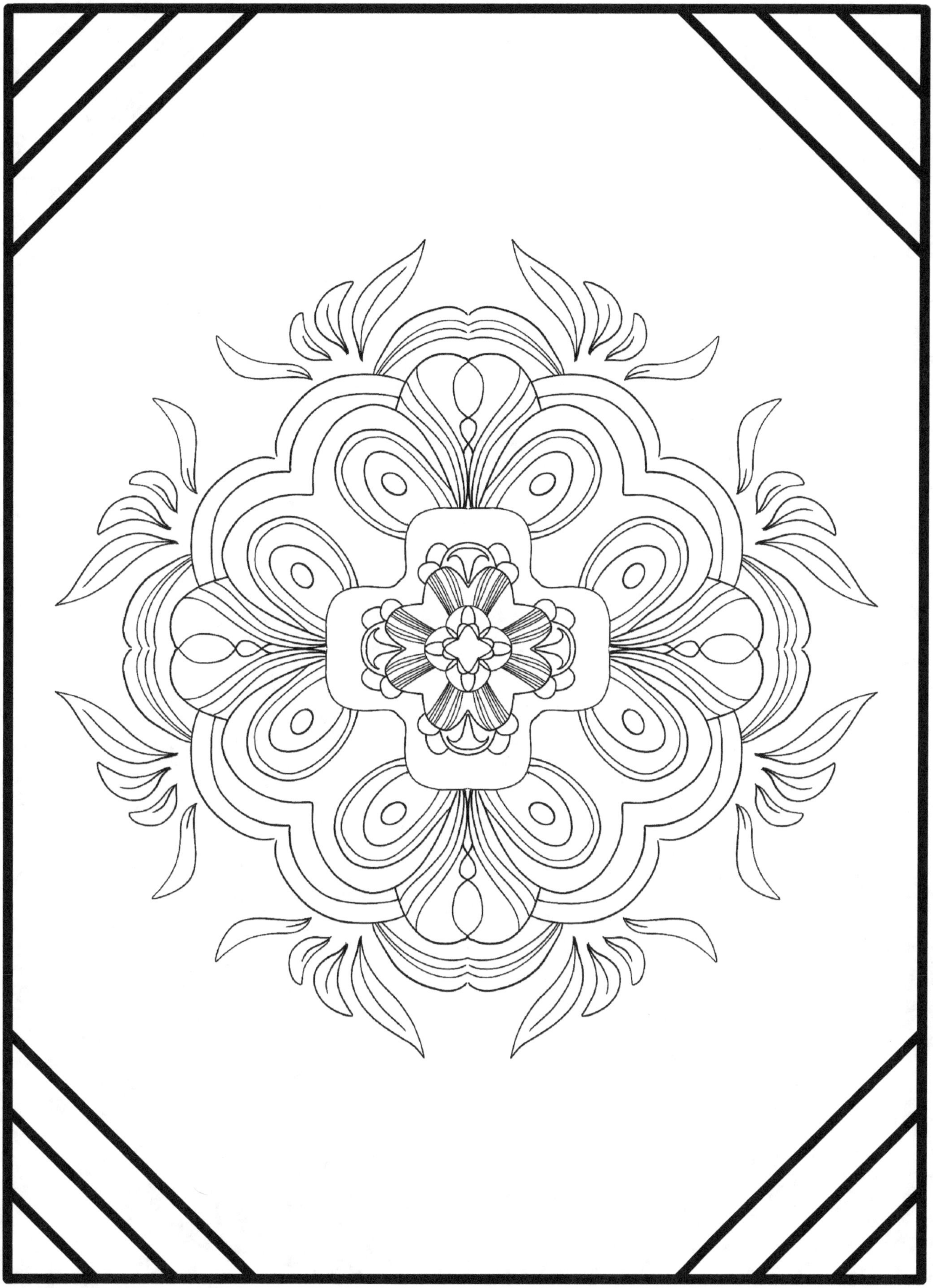

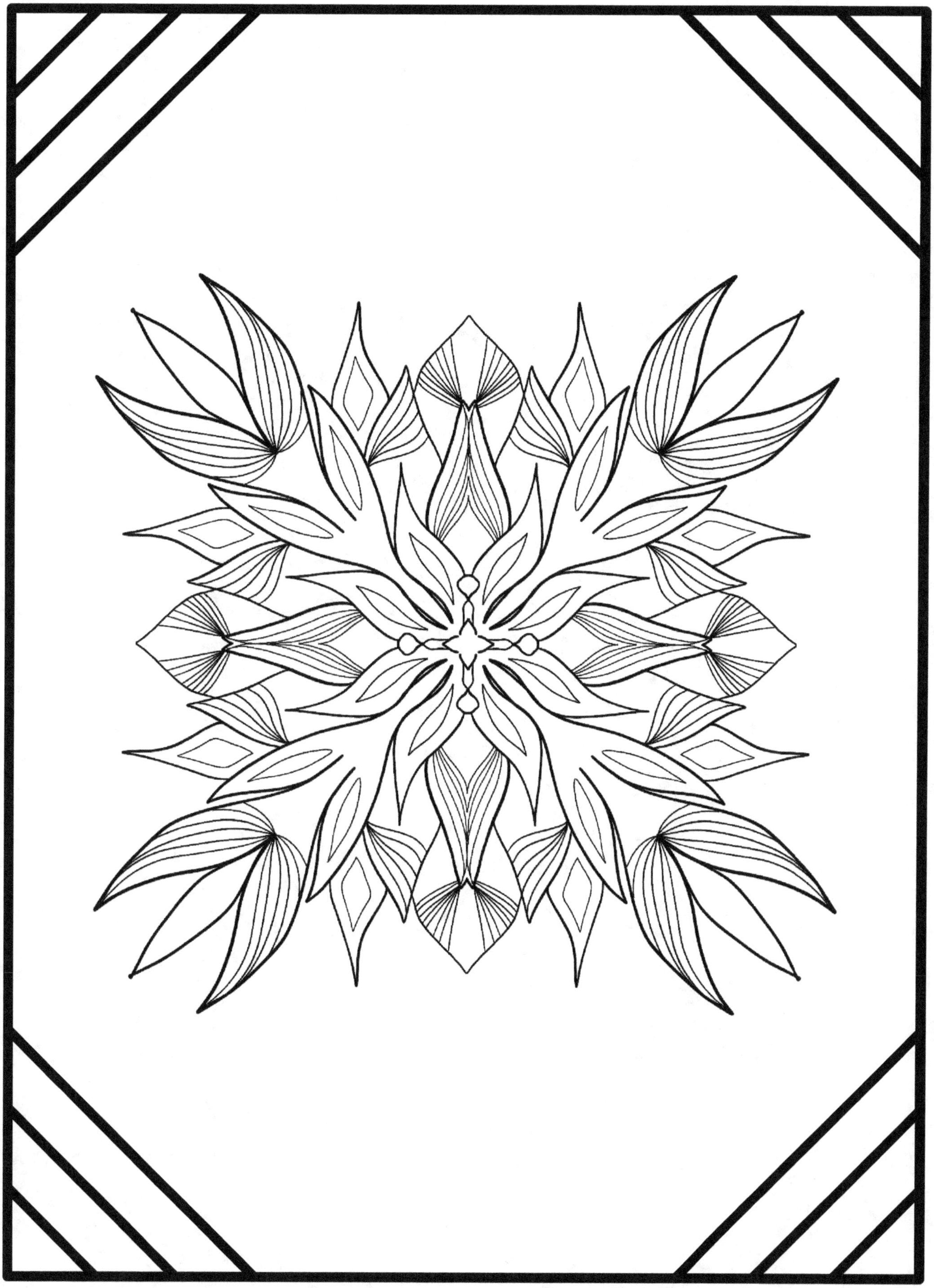

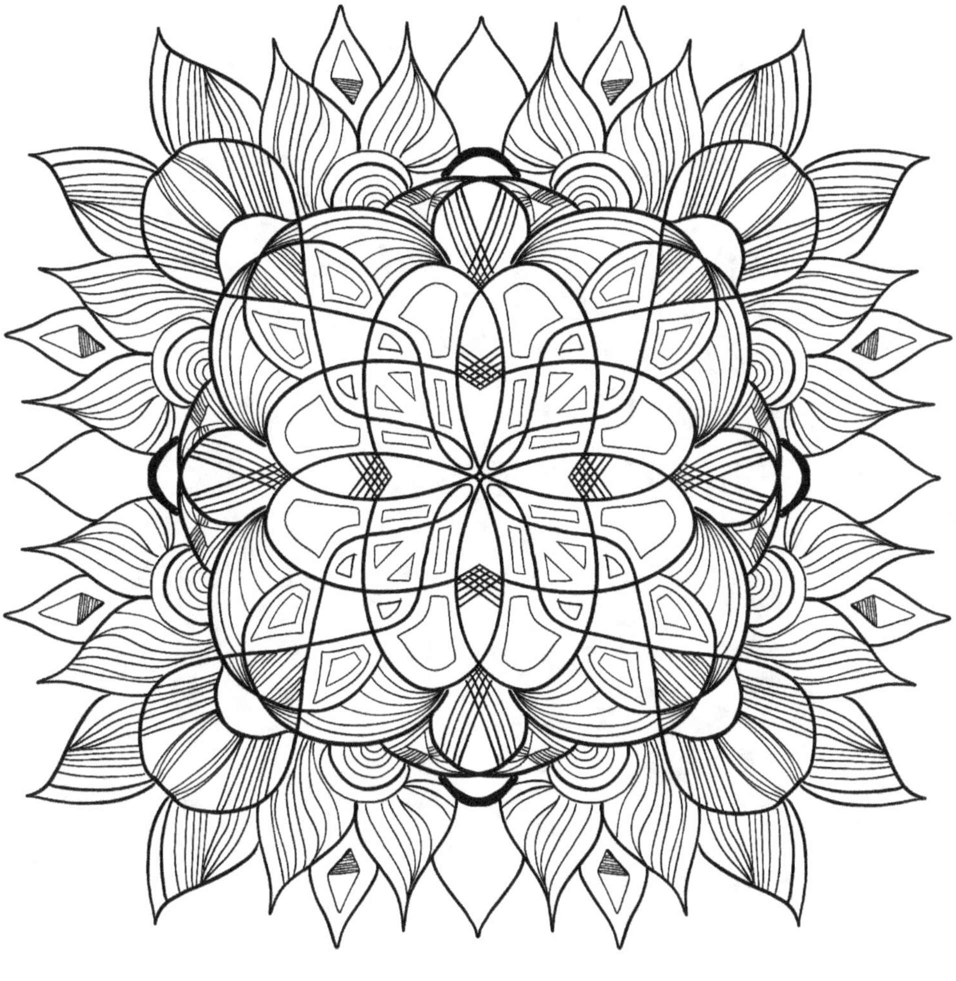

www.ingramcontent.com/pod-product-compliance
Lightning Source LLC
Chambersburg PA
CBHW081148170526
45158CB00009BA/2772
* 9 7 8 1 0 7 0 1 9 5 4 0 7 *